To
Pat & Bob
Thanks for supporting
Lincolnville Jazz & Poetry
Dr. R. Som.

More Than
A Simple Kiss

Sketches of Life and Love

The Poetry of

R. B. Batie

i

Published in 2007 by
Geneva Publishing Co.
P.O. Box 1926
Lutz, FL 33548-1926

No claim to original U.S. Government works
Printed in the United States of America

International Standard Book Number-10: 0-9790482-0-6
International Standard Book Number-13: 978-0-9790482-0-3
Library of Congress Card Number: 2006909442

Trademark Notice:
Product or corporate names may be trademarks or registered
trademarks, and are used only for identification and explanation
without intent to infringe.

Library of Congress Cataloging-in-Publication Data

Batie, R. B. Geneva Publishing Co.
More Than a Simple Kiss
ISBN: 978-0-9790482-0-3
LCCN: 2006909442

Table of Contents

First Poems

Lost in the Sauce	1
Freedom in the mood swing	1
M.L. King	2
What might have been	2
Those Eyes	3
Gauging Love	4
Haikus	5
Oh Ella, My Love	6
Morning message on an answering machine	6
What is there 2 say of love	7
My Funny Valentine	8

The Art of Loving

The Vows	11
Computer Love	12
My Honey Valentine	13
Am I?	14
Warm thoughts of U	15
"My Room"	15
EN THIS PRECARIOUS LOVE AFFAIR	16
Cosmic Bliss	17
The Beauty of Oneness	17
A Place	18
LOVE YOU BABY!	19
Missing Elements	20
Afternoon@Linda's	20
Dying Love	22
Want U all the time	23
This Flaming Heart	24
The Axis	25
This Time	28
You used to love me	31
@#$%&*! (At)	33
My Queen of Hearts	34

A Simple Kiss   35
Gorgeous   37

Sketches of Life

I Survived   39
Dawn of a New Day   40
Primetime News   41
A Blues for Dina   43
JANICE...   44
TRACY   45
Bobby # 23   47
Finishing Grad School   47
Heaven and Earth   48
Bridges   49
Finding Frank L.   50
Tick... Tick...   51
Younger Daze   52
Revolution   53

Sweet Sorrow in the Morning

Losing Mom   55
Remembering Frank   56
To Ernest and Debbie on the loss of their son Bryan   57
For Darius Turhan Batie   57
16 April 16   58
Another Summer Without You   59
For Elise   60
Our Heart and Soul   61
Brown Shoes   62
Our Grief in Five Stages   63
New Again, Blue Again   65
Four-Get-U-Not   66

Gestation of a New Life

Gestation of a New Life	69
WRT: Gestation of a new life	70
A flashy salesman	71
Waiting for Spring	73
The Trouble with This Place	74
What happened to my dream	75
Sundays	76
Tax Time	77
Princess Di	78
DRIFTING	79
St. Cyprian's Children	80

INTRODUCTION

I started writing poetry in the late summer of 1986 while taking a creative writing course at the University of Maryland's European Division in Heidelberg Germany. I am not sure why I took ENGLISH 294 because I struggled in the course and didn't get a very good grade, However, I wrote some poems that all my classmates liked. The first poem I wrote was called "Lost in the Sauce". It was an eleventh hour attempt to turn in something for my homework assignment. It really was the first, and I was lost in the world of creative writing.

Poetry excited me long before ENGLISH 294. The most impressionable poets I grew up listening to and reading were "The Last Poets". Their poems were absolutely off the chain. I was about 12 or so. The language they used, the rhyme, the subjects and the way they put it all together was pure genius. I could recite all of their stuff. To this day, I still remember quite a bit of it. Their poetry spoke to me on a lot of levels. I became more aware politically and personally more aware of my blackness during the turbulent 60's. This was the time of the civil rights movement, Afros and dashikis, black power, "Black is Beautiful", and the Viet Nam war. When I eventually got around to writing my own poems, the Last Poets were long gone. I was able to find a couple of books that told their story at a swap meet in Harlem many years later.

I have always loved deep lyrics and spectacular prose which is why my favorite author is Toni Morrison. I think I have read and/or listened to all of her work including her Nobel Prize for literature acceptance speech. I am also a big fan of Maya Angelou's poetry and, lately, Ms. Jill Scott.

Once I was bitten with the poetry bug in 1986, I encouraged my son and daughter to write, too. My daughter was nine when she wrote her first poem about Dr. Martin Luther King. It is included in the "First Poems" section. My son was 14 when he wrote his first poem called "The world is yours, the world is mine". It is also included in the "First Poems" section. My daughter turned out to be a prolific poet and my son's a musician who writes and composes his own music. No music is included in this book however, you can check out his website at www.batie.net.

I think writing is contagious. Sometimes I write a poem to my wife and she writes one back to me or sometimes she writes me one and I respond to hers with one of my own. There are a couple of those poems in here, too.

I didn't start writing poems with the thought of publishing. I was just having conversations with myself or with someone else. These conversations were rants, vents, personal perspectives, decompression, anti-stressing, a sedative for pain, wishful thinking and or creative monologue. Over the years I kept track of most of them and finally decided to do something with them for my milestone 50th birthday party. I chickened out and chose to read a few at the party instead of publishing the entire package. Everyone loved what I read so I thought now was a good time to take the final step and publish.

Words speak to me at the most inconvenient times, like in the middle of the night. Sometimes they come on like a flood and I have to get up and write. But, I've learned over the years, if I don't get up and write, the words will not be there when the sun comes up, only fragments of what was destined to be some really great stuff. So, I keep a pen and pad bedside. At other times, words come when I'm driving. I have missed a lot of them but I have also had to pull over and write or scribble at the stoplight. Most of the pieces were written in just a few minutes probably no more than 10 or 15. Occasionally I will go back and do some word-smithing as an after-thought but usually not much.

So what exactly is poetry to me? Poetry is vividly capturing a thought, a moment or feelings and expressing the same in as few written words as possible. God has blessed me with many gifts and talents. Writing poetry is another one. I hope you find some here that you enjoy, and that you are encouraged to write some of your own. I have enjoyed sharing mine with you. Many thanks!

--RB[2]

<u>Acknowledgements</u>

Thanks to God most high

To my family and friends who contributed their time and talent to this project and helped make the dream a reality, especially:

LaFern K. Batie a.k.a. LKB,
who is a contributing poet, my conscience, editor, voice of reason, sounding board, best friend and life partner.

Many thanks to the other contributing poets, your work added sugar and spice:

Janice D. Batie, a.k.a. JDB.
Colise J. Frazier, a.k.a. CJF
Robert T. Batie, a.k.a. RTB
Rontel Batie, a.k.a. RB.

Also many thanks to the other hearts and minds, whose input was invaluable:

Selma Robinson-Ayers
Charnessa Brown
Charles Harbor-Clark
Vanessa Henley
Paul Vazquez Jr.
Gregory H.

<u>Dedication</u>

My Parents:

My Mother, Helen G^2 Gordon, the light of my life and one of the greatest examples of hard work and prudent living imaginable. The queen of "make ends meet", always encouraging me to do my best and always there when I needed her. She taught me responsibility and showed me a love I never knew existed. I miss her everyday.

My father, Robert B. Batie Sr. who loved me from day 1, as long as I can remember, he always set the standards to live by. He taught me almost everything I know about being a man. I still lean on his lessons.

My surrogate mom, Lucille Batie who was on the front line in my life, augmenting the lessons I learned from Helen and RB, with some of her own, special brand of loving and living.

The rest of my village.

More Than A Simple Kiss

First Poems

Lost in the Sauce

Lost in the sauce am I,
             a man without an alibi,
        never knowing
           where I'm going
      while the world passes me by.
Lost in the sauce I've been,
              since I can't remember when,
     from childhood
          TO MANHOOD
      it must surely be a sin.
Order and perfection were never my direction.
      Profound inspiration was not part of the equation,
          Why must I always be… like noodles of
spaghetti…
      Lost in the sauce.

RB[2]

Freedom in the mood swing

      One shining soul,
      plays hide and seek
      against streams of consciousness.
      Dare I ask,
      what sweet sorrow is there
      alone, in the morning?
      chill... obsession... faith... rejoice?
      Mischievous innovative dialogue,
      Can't dance to this pantomime of
      cat battles,
      when the sun comes down to
      oneness in two, home fries and
      the past in present.

      RB[2]

M.L. King

M.L. King was a very wise man
He had to watch himself for where ever he should stand
His name would change for where ever he'd go
His name was not Martin, his name would be Negro,
Though no one was different but the skin colors apart
Martin didn't care all his love was from his heart
We're not all free from this terrible task
Let us sing of joy that is all we should ask.

JDB, (age 9)

What might have been

If time were on my side
and the sandbox had more room
I'd take U 4 a ride
in a hot air balloon.

I'd come at U in slow-motion,
like a hunter stalks its prey,
and 1, by 1, by 1,
peel every layer away.

In space that smells of incense
that's lit by candlelight,
I'd lift your spirit to the sky
like an osprey soaring in flight.

I'd extend my slender fingers
across your honey colored skin,
with water flowers caress U,
touch places you've never been.

As your thoughts ascend to heaven
and your pent-up rivers flow
I'd delicately tie U
into a perfect bow.
RB[2]

Those Eyes

I often wonder to my dismay,
If I dare ask what would she say?
Where did she get those eyes like that?
I bet she stole them from a cat.

So large and soft they sparkle bright,
I wonder how they'd look at night?
Hazel, brown and emerald green.
I sometimes see them in my dreams.

If eyes are windows to the soul,
I see she has a heart of gold.
If eyes reflect back what they see,
I see she thinks the world of me.

Those crowded fantasies in my mind,
the smell of jasmine, the taste of wine.
Out there somewhere, there must be,
a cat, who has no eyes to see.
RB[2]

Gauging Love

Can love be measured in leaps and bounds,
or is it measured by how "I love you" sounds?
Is it measured by a radio telescope,
peering endlessly towards the edge of the universe
or simply measured by a baby's birth?

What of the distance between planet and sun?
What of the good times and frolicking fun?
Can love be measured by the width of a smile,
or more than 5000 feet that makes up a mile?

Let me count the ways...
It could be measured in hours or days
or the colors of sky with its blues and its grays.
I wonder if it is by the beats of a heart,
or the distance between lovers when they are apart?

Would one use a Sextant to determine its arc
or convert it to Kelvins and equate to its spark?
Might it be bundled and weighed by the ounce,
or would large karats be a much better source?

Can it be measured by that thing we do?
The intimate reactions between me and you.
How about gauging the look in her eyes,
they sparkle so brightly with the joy of surprise.

Fifty ways to read your lover...
Enigmatic feelings no analysis can uncover
The magic of something new being discovered.
Whatever your yardstick, however your fun
True love is measured by the power of one.

RB[2]

Haikus

Chloe
New baby Chloe
Demure, petite, two pounds cute
Her heart weighs a ton.
LKB

Inhale
Love in full blossom
Pollinates the Springtime air
Fills my lungs with joy.
LKB

Teeth
Grind them in my sleep,
Must be my subconscious thoughts
gnawing on my brain.
LKB

Wisdom
Don't take my wisdom
From four corners of my mouth
I ache for knowledge
LKB

Shell fish
Luscious crustaceans
Causes swelling, welts and hives
I react badly
RB^2

Solitude
In a crowded room
no one feels my pain except
me, myself and I.
RB^2

Teeth
Gleaming pearly whites
hide behind generous lips
I brush twice a day.
RB^2

WRG Haiku # 7
I like your juice, too
Honey brown sugar and sweet spice
Pour me another cup.
RB^2

Oh Ella, My Love

Our love has gone through many twists and turns,
We were disheartened by this flame that burns
We share a love that is filled with joy and pain
And stayed together as our love grew and stretched and
strained

We held on tight through many frightful nights
Lay side by side and watched the sunrise with delight
Your counsel is the strength my spirit needs
To keep this fiery soul on an even keel

Oh Ella, won't you take my hand?
And together before the altar we will stand
And speak the vows of holy matrimony
For God and all the world to see
R.B.

Morning message on an answering machine

Good morning my ebony princess,
Your smile is the smile of a thousand African violets.
I am always pleased when you share it with me.
If life, or love or work get you down today,
I will lift your spirit with a hug from my strong arms.
Let me nourish and protect your fragile body from
the evils of this world.
Bathe you in the waters of the Nile,
And message your honey brown skin with
fragrant oils from the dollar store.
Think warm thoughts of you until...
Our eyes meet in the autumn sunset
Call me!
RB[2]

What is there 2 say of love

What is there 2 say of love?

When all there is to say, has been said.

Unless we take some menial thing

And equate it to metaphor, or simile,

            or some other abstractions.

The fad of the day,

      a sound byte or

          some cute cliché.

Love will always be

          in fashion.

Love for her… him… the convenience of

      words whispered in dark places,

            by candle light?

What is there to say?

When words are cheapened by their sound,

      only valued if they R written down.

No words can describe my love 4-U

        Love is not what a person says,

     Love is what a person does.

You wanna love me, then do it! 'cause

Words, limit the love and our

      realm of responsibility.

RB[2]

My Funny Valentine

You are my world of endless possibilities
Your presence always seems to calm
this raging storm inside of me.

Our conversation flows so soft and smooth
Like a phonograph's needles sliding towards its first groove
Your voice is the sound of jazz that ubiquitously soothes.

A backward glance replays how we first met by chance.
My pain ran deep, my soul cried out for just one dance.
The joy you bring creates a delicate balance.

What is this gravity that makes me want to run to you?
Why do I hesitate, why do I not pursue?
Has my Spinderella lost her other shoe?

Your beauty is much deeper than the skin
Warm thoughts of lovin' you would make the cherubs grin
Our friendship is a lifeline on which I can depend.

Though our encounters are few and far between,
The faint glow of candlelight can always be seen.
Is it fireflies across a distant stream
or is the light left on to wake me from this dream?

RB²

Untitled

Your email has warmed my heart
like elements of a toaster
next to a pop tart.

Those words quietly spoken
cut across a blue screen
with sunny yellow characters
arrived in packets unbroken.

Though we are miles apart
at the speed of light we embrace
through the magnetism that
emanates the warmth of your smile.

Those bits, mathematically arranged
modulate, demodulate,
create a connection, hard to explain.
The transformation is sensual.

R.B^2

The World is Yours the World is Mine

The world is yours the world is mine
If we understand that we will be just fine
One thing I know in this world to be true
Since we own the world it is up to me and you.

We cannot ignore or pretend to be blind
We must save the world in our lifetime
When we love the world it loves us back
The world is ours and that's a fact.

RTB (age 14)

The Art of Loving

The Vows

I pledge my blood, my love to thee
From here until infinity
Me for you and you for me.

A love no clock nor meter measure
A love of sweet and endless pleasure
A love my flesh and bones will treasure.

No slab or slice or chunk or shave
And nary drop of love I'll save
I'll love the still beyond the grave.

I'll love you through the storm and rain
Stay by your side through joy and pain
'til sanity does seem insane.

Come love me while the seasons last
Until my breath I draw its last
In stone, my love for thee I cast.
RB[2]

Your Dewy Love

You are my sunshine, the stars in these moonstruck eyes…
You are the hand that wipes the tears I cry…
You are my everything.

Hold on to my love and never let it go…
Say yes to my dreams when even I say no…
Believe in me.

Hear me when I tell you that this rose would
Wilt every single petal if it never could
Embrace your dewy love.

LKB

Computer Love

Computer love, new love in my life
her bits and bytes are shear delight
When I'm in her Megahertz, I feel no pain
when she retrieves my data, I nearly go insane.

She is strong in her configuration
when all others have gone
LAN, my computer love
stands alone.

Her flashing cursor smiles at me
whether night or day
I just can't get enough
of her digital display.

My keystrokes are caresses
our networks are synchronized
her clock pulse in my heart beat
the password is "my_ disguise"

Her software is exciting
she boots up right on cue
with all the languages she can speak
she knows just what to do!

IF: she feels this magic
THEN: let our feelings flow
GOTO: the place in memory
WHERE: 2 hearts compute as 1!
RB^2

My Honey Valentine

You're my honey Valentine
Slanted smile, intelligent eyes
the love I feel is no surprise, and
even Ray Charles can see that.

You are my heart, my lucky charm
my fantasies all soft and warm
when I'm away please think of me
as I so often do, when I'm without you.

Those precious memories I play again and again
they warm my heart from end to end.
I've placed your picture on my desk,
I greet your smile with baited breath.

It's brightened up my office space
and gives my soul its warm embrace,
'though valentines R overrated
and those cherubs are insane assassins,
U-R Spectacular!!

RB^2

Am I?

Whenever you think of me
these are the things I hope you see
Your best friend and confidante
Your sounding board when you
need to vent.
What ever you want me to be
Odd-job, handyman, jack-of-all-trades
Your cool spot on a hot summer day
The best lover you've ever had.
The one that makes you laugh
when you're feeling sad
A warm blanket on a cold night
an umbrella when it rains
a comfort zone
when you need some time alone.
Food for thought when you're
mentally stressed.
Prozac when you're depressed
Sunshine on a rainy day
silence when you have nothing to say
Your therapist!
Your rock to lean on or hide under
a safe place when you fear the lightening and thunder
your partner in crime
your peaches and cream
your sexiest thoughts
your wettest dreams.
Your one stop shopping
your cutest pair of shoes
a smile on your face
when you get the blues.
Your fun spot, your G spot
when you are under the gun
your one and only,
your only one.

RB[2]

Warm thoughts of U

I close my eyes and think of you
I lick my lips and taste your kiss
I feel the breeze, it's your embrace
I touch myself, it's your caress
I close my eyes and think of you
and colors burst like fireworks
I wrap you up in tender arms
and press you to my body's warmth.
warm thoughts of you course through my veins
run through my heart, dance on my brain
'til sanity does seem insane
You are a mystery, an enigma, and algorithm
my mathematical capabilities cannot comprehend
Does $H + A = I$ or is it Y?
Tell me of that space which brings you insatiable joy
and I will touch you there and soothe your pain.
RB[2]

"My Room"

I want you in my room,
to fill it with the music of your laughter,
the sweetness of your perfume.

Eight corners of this comfort zone,
the boundaries of my private space,
beckons your presence to embrace.

You'd make the walls so happy,
the furniture would smile,
the mirror, silver and exact
reflects your elegant style.

The bed would sing a song of joy,
and all the candles glow.
the fan would spin so dizzily
and no one else would know...

The pleasures of this space,
Except, you and I,
dancin' on the ceiling!!
RB[2]

EN THIS PRECARIOUS LOVE AFFAIR

En this precarious love affair,
i soar 2 heights, where Oxygen is light and rare.
We want 2 exhale, 2 breathe again,
n spaces where we can be 4-ever friends.

My feelings r sometimes hard 2 share,
cause I've been there,
n deep dark wells of pain,
where the rainbow no longer chases the rain.

Memories of your tenderness dance across my mind,
the curve of your hips, the pucker of your lips
the dew on your petals is as sweet as wine
we're entangled like the vines.

Me lovin u,|,u nivol eM
(u lovin me)
that's an awesome responsibility.
I fear hurting u
and though I never intend 2,
1-day it may come tru.

Is it really up 2 me?
Can a butterfly, change the stripes on a bumble bee?
Without your touch I'd B lost at sea.

RB^2

The Beauty of Oneness

The beauty of oneness, oneness in two,
is that each separate part is honest and true.
The two stand together for common a cause,
they both can support without question or clause.

Whether united or working apart,
 they are always together in spirit, in heart.
Though, one clearly leads and one often follows,
both voices are heard, no words must be swallowed.

The beautiful creation from two, equals three,
a miracle of life for all others to see.
They look to each other for protection and praise,
and challenge one another to the standards they've raised.

No one hides in shadows of the other one's wings,
they soar side by side in the sun, in the rain.
The beauty of oneness is in the love that they share,
unselfish, undying, and genuine care.

RB^2

Cosmic Bliss

You have worked your magic on my humble being
Stabilizing my insecurities with the curve of your smile
Your fingers are on the pulse of my emotions
Every heartbeat is for you.

Your eyes have pierced my Soul
Driving my desire to the edge of the envelope
I gravitate to the place where our inertia collide…
All the while, I am gasping for breath.
RB^2

A Place

I search for a place that is honest and true
where unconditional love is nothing new.
It flows like cool water from a sulfur spring
and everybody there are just doing their own thing.

I search for a space that's not too loose and not too tight
where the gloves and the shoes and feelings fit just right.
Where the music is jazz and the place is not filled with smoke
so I don't have to cuss or cough or choke.

The food is high protein and low calorie
And nobody fights even though they sometimes disagree.
The women…the women mean what they say and say what they
mean
cause there are just too many lines I must read in between.

I want to find a location
where there's no desecration
of the flag, or the minds or David's star.
Where they never cover people in feathers or tar.

I search for a place that is warmed by sunlight
and children aren't afraid when the day turns to night
And grandmas who have shed so many tears
can just use an apron to chase away their fears.

There are very few places on this earth I know,
where your friends are friends and foes are foe.
We are all sort of mixed up and confused
clinging to material things we don't want to lose.

I found God's kingdom to be the place
where people aren't judged by gender or race.
Where patience and love and the spirits reign supreme,
and we live by faith in his loving grace.

RB[2]

LOVE YOU BABY!

LOVE YOU BABY!
Always have, always will,
Loving you is such a thrill,
sends my body into chills

LOVE YOU BABY!
Beyond a shadow of a doubt,
From Mt. Everest, shout it out,
It's you I can't live without!

LOVE YOU BABY!
Always and forever
'til the last day of never
It's really not that clever.

LOVE YOU BABY!
Wish you only knew,
that this love is really true,
and can never do without you.

LOVE YOU BABY!
Without malice or forethought,
This love can't be sold or bought
In spite of many times we've fought.

LOVE YOU BABY!
In the sun and the rain,
in spite of all the pain,
until I go insane.

LOVE YOU BABY!
Yesterday, today and tomorrow,
with no regrets or sorrows,
With all the LOVE that God allows,
LOVE YOU BABY!

RB^2

Missing Elements

A rock to lean on, to hide under, to support my weariness
A strong arm to elevate me to transport me to places
unknown
Rain to cleanse the parched heart, to renew my spirit
Wind to blow away my worries, to whisk me afar to dry the
tears
Fire back into my life, to ignite the emptiness

Missing elements…
LKB

Afternoon@Linda's

The afternoon our eyes met
again for the first time
I wanted to see just what lay
Beneath the warmth and tenderness
That surrounds you.

I remember every moment
the look, the hug, the laughter, all so familiar, yet new
your silent eyes emanated infinite possibilities
my thoughts wandered to passion
and what your kisses would taste like.

I had missed them so since grade 2.
Had I had more courage, I might have known

We moved our universe to the porch, then curbside
I did not want to leave the comfort of your company.

RB[2]

Stellar Evening in Your Arms

Honey you excited me in ways that cannot be defined
like the rush of white water rafting,
or a roller coaster ride turning me upside down
hopelessly lost and captivated by the sounds.
Arrest me, impress me, undress me,
    with a look that says it all,
        made me feel 10 feet tall.
       Rode me, ride me, untied me
          from a hitching post of gloom
            let me in your space,
              not to late and not too soon
                swept me up with
              your magic broom.
              Broke me down, ran me
        around
              that mulberry bush
                upon the falling
              star I wish
        The Gods have smiled on us for sure
          we shared an apple and its core
            you are my cheri amour!

             Fired me, cross-wired me
             Like a printed circuit board
            High above the clouds we soared

             I am the itch you are the scratch
               Collect me, wreck me
             Like a scattered derailed train
              I will never be the same

           Point me, disjoint me, anoint me
            In a way that serves you best
                I will never rest
              Not until you are there
       Standing at the top of ecstacy's stairs.

RB^2

                Inspired me,
               acquired me
         Brought me through the wretched storm
                cultivates a LOVE
           that chills and thrills and warms. --

Dying Love

This love is dying fast
Fading, like painted colors on an old house
Cracking, peeling and chalky, a victim
Of too many summers and winters past.

Now and then it comes up gasping for air
Only to find the tank of "O" nearly depleted
Suffocating from thoughtless comments, no offense
Searching in the dark for understanding, but none is there.

This emergency is placed in intensive care
EKGs, CPR, and IVs
Polyvinyl umbilical cord its only lifeline
On a respirator with tubes stuck everywhere.

To keep alive this dying soul's a lonely cause
The lingering will only cause more pain
A wounded dog is put out of its misery
So let it die without another pause.

If parting is made better, the time is now
The crystal ball holds no future here
So let us part while we still smile
But when, where and why,
I don't know how.

RB^2

Want U all the time

I want U all the time
Can't you feel my vibes emanating?
           The earthquake of my emotions
                      Their thunderous aftershocks beating
                                Against your Richter scale?
                                     Still want you all the time
                                          You are my sexual
                                               healing
                                                    My sun
                                               goddess, my
                                               beam of light

Stretching across the cosmos
           Of my emotions
                      You are my joy slightly off center
                                Warmed by its core
                                     When ever I see U or touch U
                                          or slumber between
                                               Streams of
                                                    consciousness

My want for U is ever present
You are my high-protein-low-cal-slim-slow
           Brown-sugar-chocolate-with-nuts
                      My sweet tooth
                                Want U all the time
                                     Far more than I could have ever
                                          imagined
                                          At this juncture
                                               Far beyond the
realm of my insensitivities
The far side of fire
           Kindled by my unquenchable desire for U
                      Want U more, than silence
                                Much more than rain
                                     My soul, in silence screams
                                          your name
                                               With every heartbeat
RB²   I will never stop
                                               wanting U.

This Flaming Heart

This flaming heart
Will never die
It loves you so
I always will.
No H_2O
or oxygen
depleted space
can cause
it to
surrender
its vigilant state.
The nebulous dance
of heat and light
intrinsic
to
flames like you and I
are intertwined.
This flaming
heart is yours
to
kindle
and tender
and stoke
'til time has passed
and I have
drawn
my last gaze into your eyes,
my breath
and
one final
thought
of
loving
you.

RB[2]

The Axis

The one who holds the Axis,
on which my world spins,
is always there when I need her
time and time again.

This world is not perfect,
this axis is not straight,
so when I need to lean on
her she does not hesitate.

I've found the strength of Atlas,
the wisdom of the gods,
the patience of the one called Job,
the wonders of the stars.

The one who holds the axis,
on which my world spins,
has a heart that knows the
seasons, from summer to the spring.

Her love's a constellation,
scattered across the universe,
her soul is in the right place,
right down to earth.

The ways she makes me feel,
the things she does to me,
I hope this magnetic
field equates to infinity.

RB^2

Love Was Never My Intent

Love was never my intent,
Straight up feelings twisted and bent
Not touching the lives
For which it was meant

Was not / was supposed to be
A quiescent state of mind to me
Has effervescences'd, most joyously

Oh feel the fire of desire
I am consumed in its flame
And no one else is to blame
And no one should be a shamed

I have tried to hide it, deny it,
Disguise, evade and camouflage it
Must take my whipping like a man
Tired of getting beat up at love's hand
Another heartache I must withstand

30 wondrous days to go
'til my lover is no more
beaming to a distant shore

Wouldn't let us part this way
I take the time to boldly say,
I love you, no string attached.

RB[2]

Alone At Night

Sometimes when I'm alone at night
My mind takes off on sensuous flights
I lay across this empty bed
Warm thoughts of you race through my head

Run through my heart, dance on my brain
It causes excruciating pain
Not to have you here with me
Only your love can set me free

My heart's so pumped it skips a beat,
To think of us between the sheets,
An exercise I must repeat,
I must repeat to be complete

Sometimes when I'm alone at night
Warm thoughts of you make things alright
To know that you're somewhere out there
To think you really, really care

And when I'm really feeling low
I visit you on video
I view your movements and your sounds
And what I feel is so profound

Although its only been a week
Resistance is low and spirits are weak
I pace myself for the long wait
Until we have another date

Sometimes when I'm along at night,
Stayed up to watch Arsenio
I hunger for a late night snack
Of Haagen Das and pistachios

I read your letters one by one
They bring back memories of our fun
The jokes, the songs, and thunder runs
The games we played while dancing in the sun

More vivid than the morning calm
Reflects the nucleus of your charm
The fire is out and taps is played
I dream of things our love has made.
RB[2]

This Time

I've told you of those lonely nights
And asked about this love deferred
I'll tell you of this empty heart
Filled with a love that you deserve

I'd love to spend this time with you
Caress your lips and kiss your thighs
And count the ways to breathless joy
Cast wishes against a starry sky

To hold your beautiful hand by dear
Against my heart and to my cheek
Read you your horoscope each day
Sit next to you in church each week

And when we dine, I'll pick the wine
Dom Perignon or chardonnay
Serve pasta on a crystal dish
And scampi cooked your special way

I'll listen to your thrilling tales
Of lovers lost and broken dreams
Of futures bright and hope's delight
While floating on a wind swept sail

I'll walk with you for miles and miles
Until your weary feet are sore
I'll rub them down and tickle them
Until you beg me "please no more!"

I could go on and speculate
On how I'd spend this time with you
I'll let your conscious be your guide
I'm sure you can imagine too!

RB[2]

Before the Well Runs Dry

Before the well runs dry
I will open up for all to see
The joy and pain that resides deep inside of me
This raging sea, these stormy nights
Before the well runs dry.

I will pass on the secrets of my survival
My magnificent boyish style
That makes the girls and women smile
To sooth their fears and dry their tears
Before the well runs dry.

I will count the stars one by one
And rearrange the universe
To meet your exact specification
I will do these things without hesitation
Before the well runs dry.

Before the music stops and movement cease
Before we find that total peace
I will share with you a love supreme
Discovered while wandering through your dreams.

Before the ink dries on this page
Before I go off on a rant and rave
Before we hit that final stage
Oh well, the well… ran dry…

RB^2

IF you need to know

If you need to know if someone does… I do.
If you need to know a reason why,
It's just because you' re you.

If you need to know how long I will,
Well, 'til old Betsy comes over the hill
Until Happy Valley has its last chill

If you need to know how much
A whole heap X a lot X a bunch

If you need to know
The "with what I measure"
You are my one and only treasure
And truly it is all my pleasure

To let you know
with all my heart
how much I love you so!

RB^2

You used to love me

You used to love me
Notes sweet with songs of love
Dear J
I hope you have a nice day
You are the sun, moon and stars
To my very existence
Your name spells perfect...
Love Me
True words from you
I'd rush to my e-mail
Or fall over the phone
Knowing your words world heal the day's wounds
Now I find me
Mending my own heart

In the quiet
Of the middle of the night
A kiss on my forehead
Rang "I love you" louder than church bells
Now tears flow heavy
As I lay alone
With only sorrow to caress my face
Like the Nile river
Drenching me in my sorrow
Coldness fills my bed
Nothing and no one
To keep my soul warm
When for years you were my comfort
You used to love me

Nothing could keep you from me
A look in your eye
Spoke in a million voices
And told me I was safe in your arms
A smile to capture the most perfect Kodak moment
Set me free from past heartaches

A stay in the middle of 3am
Or high noon
Cuz you couldn't sleep
Or your day wasn't complete
Without seeing my face
A world full of beauty that was ours
You used to love me

Now I sit here in sadness
Wondering what has gone wrong
The sights and sound of love gone
And my cries for you
Fall on ears
That pretends not to care
Not a good bye
But simply disappear
Leaving me speechless
With so much to say
Wanting to communicate again with you
With soft touches
But you've not spoken to me in so long
You've forgotten our sign language
Yesterday
Was so full of hopes and dreams
A beautiful future
But you passed me on the road and simply
Honked your horn to say hello...
You used to love me

JDB

@#$%&*! (At)

We'll never be closer than we are today
Cause soon your love will drift away
Two ships that docked in port by night
It wasn't wrong it wasn't right
The heart felt joy was dynamite
You left a song my heart could sing
And now I'm sure of just one thing
@#$%&*!

To celebrate my feelings true
With these two hearts we couldn't lose
You brought me back from loneliness
my heart and soul was so restless
You calmed the storm inside of me
And now it is time to set me free
But just one thing before you go
There's something that you've got to know
@#$%&*!

We celebrate the times we had
Cause losing us will be so sad
And yet it makes my heart feel glad
To know that you have found the strength
To move on down your chosen path
It's simple if you do the math,
That 1x 1 is 1
The love we have stays on my mind
And it was so much fun
And @#$%&*!

You taught me things I never knew
A guy could learn a lot from you
You are so interesting and smart
I know you are my queen of hearts
And beautiful without a doubt
You make me want to twist and shout
But bet you'll never figure out
How much I loved you so!

RB^2

My Queen of Hearts

We'll never be closer than we are today
I feel your love drifting away
Two ships that docked in port for life
You nearly were the perfect wife
The heart felt joy was dynamite
You left a song my heart could sing
That made me sure of just one thing
My love for you

To celebrate my love so true
With our two hearts we couldn't lose
You brought me back from emptiness
my heart and soul was in distress
You calmed the storm inside of me
And now it is time to set me free
But just one thing before you go
There's something that you've got to know
How much, I love you so

We celebrate the times we had
Cause losing us will be so sad
And yet it makes my heart feel glad
To know that you have found the strength
To move on down your chosen path
It's simple if you do the math
That 1x 1 is 1
The love we had stays on my mind
And it was so much fun

You taught me things I never knew
A guy could learn a lot from you
You are so interesting and smart
I know you are my queen of hearts
And beautiful without a doubt
You make me want to twist and shout
But bet you'll never figure out
How much I loved your smile

RB[2]

A Simple Kiss

A simple kiss
Sets my soul on fire
Like holding the sun in the palm of my hand
Whispering to him with my eyes
You are wonderful in my site
I have known you as long as I could grasp the concept of time
An eternity to me
Maybe the sun, the moon and the stars
Aligned themselves this night
To alter the world
Change destinies
To create a compatibility
To bring you to me
This man
Who creates shock waves
Of a devastating capacity through my spine
Each and every time he smiles my way
His heartbeat is like that of a drum
Heard from a distance
In a far off land
And I can't help but feel his rhythm
And lose myself in his sound

Can it be?
This man's vibes are for me?
Sending pulses though my veins
With his touch
Waiting, wanting, wishing,
For that day when
Sweat soaked bodies
Lay in a blissful state
Hypnotized by nothing less
Than the most beautiful
Earth shaking movements known to man
This man

Butterflies take residence
In the pit of my stomach
Fluttering
Taking hold off my thoughts

More Than A Simple Kiss
Conquering the path
From brain to mouth
And I… am speechless
In his presence

This man
On site
Makes mountains move
And waters shift, with his gift
By just being, who he is,
Perfect... And how can I compare
To the purity of his Air
When all I want to be is the very life he breathes
His everything
The landline to his lifeline
The warmth to his sunshine

The sun, the moon and the stars
will align themselves for me
And this prophesy will be
More than a distant dream
In a far off land
Conceived from a dreamer
With no real concept of reality
Within the scope
Of endless possibility
Of he and I
Magical poetry
Written in the sky
In another space and time
Where I will be his
And we can defy time
The beginning and the end
The start and the finish
we'll recreate a million times
And one little wish
A movement that started
With one simple kiss
The thought of a treasure
I cannot dismiss
This man…

JDB

Gorgeous

Baby, when I say you're gorgeous
I mean you are more than just pretty
You emanate a magnetism
That is warm and tender
It means you are the real sweet thing
And not a pretender.

When I say gorgeous, gorgeous it is twice as nice,
I mean you got a double dose
of the sugar and the spice.

Sometimes you're drop dead gorgeous
And you know I would die for you
Take you anywhere you want to go
Do anything you want to do.

Baby you're so gorgeous
You stopped the clock
You make the second hand freeze up
And the minute hand drop.

RB^2

Sketches of Life

I Survived

I have stood the tests of my times
And still I survive with a positive mind.
I survived segregation, racism and lies
I survived the brothers on the corner dealing dope and talking jive.
I survived the shattered glass that drew my blood
Bigotry and hatred that came on like the flood.
I survived my step dad beating my mom
Chasing her from home with an empty shotgun.
I survived the isolation of being the first
Black in a class I thought nothing was worst.
I survived loneliness of travel afar
I survived being threatened in a redneck bar.
I survived white lies and fairy tales
I survived incarceration when I couldn't make bail.
I survived the drug culture that took down my closest friends
Some who died and others never the same again.
I survived the Army for 22 years and 28 days
The red, white and blues that kept me enslaved.
I survived love and losing love at the height of my affection
I survived good intentions and misguided directions.
I survived being cheated and betrayed
The deck stacked against me in some devious ways
I survived losing my dad and my mom
The most familiar places all comfortable and warm.
I survived divorce and losing everything I owned
I started from scratch and built a new home.
Oh yea, I am a Cancer survivor too
I survived the mean mojo and the mad juju
I survived being back-stabbed and used.
I survived child abuse and drug misuse
I survived the thought of becoming recluse.
I survived bouts of anger and pain,
Depression and rage nearly one and the same.
I survived the colors of the rainbow
I survived the blizzards and deep, deep snow.
I survived the sunrise and misty fog
I survived being bitten by a dog.
I survived the things that generate tears
I'm surviving the aches and pains of life and living a lot of years
I'm a survivor. That's what I do.
I can surely survive with or without you,
The likes of you, the nerve of you.
I will survive until my dying day
When I have nothing left to do or say.
RB²

Dawn of a New Day

Night descends, as the sun's light ends
And black gets back in the mix again
And with the death of the sun
Our blackness becomes one
The oneness of me and you
Peeping through the Red, the White and the Blues.

Because we have no blue suede shoes
To dance to the hip hop vibe
While we express our joy and pride
In the RED, BLACK and GREEN.

Caught in another drive-by, so it seems
In the twilight of this madness
We reap the harvest of seeds sewn in sadness.

No reparations will be addressed
As we recover, only to digress
To a quiescent state of individuality
Flawed by traits in our personality
While we face this fu*ked up reality.

Of shotgun wounds and mother's tears
Of being asked to wait for years and years
We cling to love and hope this weather clears
As breaking dawn erases all our fears.

To those who perpetrate this fraud
Will hear the silence of applause
And feel the retribution of the Lord.

Stop the madness, mellow as it may be
Heal the sadness, of strange fruit hanging from the trees
Love with gladness, for it will set you free.
Hug your neighbor as yourself
Release the grip and share the wealth
Help somebody,
      your body,
          my body,
             anybody,
For we are one.   RB[2]

Primetime News

I stare and stare in utter dismay, the games you play
How could you conceive the thought that I'd believe
The bullshit you put down with such ease
Give me a break, PLEASE.

From sea to shining sea it's all the same
A space filled with lies, deceit and shame
Those ultra violet waves you rain
Somehow you forgot I have a brain.

You must think my memory is as short as my... well, its not
I'll never forget and I've never forgot
the way you insulted me, degraded me
taunted, tricked and would not let me be.

I am so tired of "that thing you do"
satisfying yourself with shallow distractions
Giving out awards for some trivial action
Rattling sound bites like a saber.

Preying upon the masses with no self esteem
Turning their nightmares into hazy dreams
I am too mad or scared to scream
Set it and forget it.

So I've just tuned you out because you have no clout
Your sensationalized trivia falls on deaf ears
And though my heart aches for truth, I have no tears
Or time to waste digesting your fabricated fears.

I have said it once, and I won't say it again
Give me the truth and nothing but the truth.
Say it once, loud and clear, bounce it off the hemisphere
and I will hear the thing I need in order to grow
Wise in my own ways.

Distorting lies to look like the truth
Contorting the truth to feel like lies
Too self absorbed to know the difference
When will you ever stop trippin'?
Film at 11.
RB^2

Ms So Feel Ya

A spice filled spirit of
All things good.
The modern Nefertiti
The mother of
Endless possibilities,
Dreams come true &
Boundless enthusiasm!
The eye of the storm
The kalm after katrina.
A soul on ice, flaming with desire,
Laced with spice
The kid and play
The sweet ending to a perfect day.
This sista's, cool, spunky
Phat and phunky.
The bearer of truth,
The builder of hope,
White woman's dope
Black folks pride.
Earthy, Jazzy, Lovely
Voice of the meek,
The treasure, the gift
1 rich chic!
The circle of joy,
The colors of love
Purple!
The third eye, America's pie
The phenomenal woman
A jeweled rainbow,
The passion, the piece of work
The pulse of humanity
The myth, the legend
Wisdom beyond years
The blood, sweat and tear
Ubiquitous, nebulous
Indescribably delicious!
The Red, Black and Green
Stedman's queen
Harpo's dream!
Oprah!
RB[2]

A Blues for Dina

I played a blues for you,
The notes were so sad and flat
(As few as they were,)
I almost didn't know where to start.

The fat juicy notes were filled with puss
I pricked them one at a time,
Then after the intro. I noticed they sagged
with loneliness.

The song ran between scales of anguish
and misunderstanding, all low notes,
they drug on and begged the question...

Where are the bright bows and high notes
of wonderful color that used to ignite your spirit
Like a symphony?

In finding us, did you lose yourself, your way?
Will losing us resurrect your self-determination,
your spirit?

It must be hard to be trapped in
An eternal do-nothingness,
Simply decomposing.

RB^2

JANICE...

She's my one and only pearl,
Oh! How I want to protect her from the evils of this world.
She is lovely in face and form, and kind beyond her years,
but since she lost her focus, she mostly stays in tears.

The road she wants to travel, seems all good times and fun,
her bags are packed, and out the door, she's going to make
a run!
She'll blow off 'til tomorrow, what she should be doing
today,
with no education or training, a heavy price to pay.

In spite of our indifference, I've told her this before,
it doesn't mean I love you less, in fact, I love you more!
I never want to change her, or mold her to my taste.
I only want to steer her away from total waste.

She's not only attractive, she's also very smart.
The attitude that she displays is breaking all our hearts.
If she continues marking time and merely standing there,
she'll spin her wheels and waste her time and not get
anywhere.

So re-adjust your focus, set new priorities,
and all the things your heart desire will be yours
immeasurably!
Honor your mother and father, do their instructions well,
they'll never lead you wrong, and you'll avoid eternal hell.

These simple words on this sheet, I hope they touch your
heart.
Let's rebuild what we've torn down, today's a good time to
start!

Love, Dad

44

TRACY

Sad and sincere,
she faces the world without fear,
to all those would lend an ear,
she'll bleed your soul and steal your cheer.

Her creative talent exemplifies,
the depth of the ocean, the height of the sky.
Her lyrics roll out in whispers and cries,
she is killed a lil' more each time another one dies.

Head full of dreds, a very simple style,
cheeks filled with dimples, a pearly white smile,
she's probably an angel or just a love child,
I'd love to sit and talk a while.

She makes you stop and smell the rose,
you'll even take notice of your crusty toes,
or take a walk where no one else goes,
become fully exposed.

She sings about life we often overlook,
and gives back the hope that society's took,
experienced things some only read in books,
Her rhythm cooks!

RB^2

Island Life

What an amazing place to be
The tropic breeze whispers
The soft song of your name
It echoes in my heart\ and in the rain
The serene blue waters set my soul at ease
The sunset, with its brilliant smile,
Stretches out across the raging sea
The heavens and earth embrace,
In a long and tender kiss.
Fragrance of tropical flowers fill the air
For one brief moment, I did not have a care
The moon light beams
Through wiry, dancing palms,
I dream of coral kings,
Jasmine stars,
And being in your arms

RB^2

Bobby # 23

The dreams you dream
The music you hear
The message is clear
The taste and smell
of success is near

Your pace has been steady
The terrain has been rough
Your persistence has been
heavy
Your character is tough

And all through your journey
Your smile has been bright
Your eyes have the sparkle
Of excitement and delight

As you celebrate today
One score and three
Continue to strive to
Be the best you can be

Love, Dad

Finishing Grad School

As I pause in this achievement
And although I am over the hill
I see I'm in a valley
Looking at yet another thrill.

I'm humbled by the presence
Of those who inspired me
To sacrifice and be a blessing
For all others to see.

I strive to set the example
For my daughter and my son
To have them know in life's
battles
Some are lost and some are won.

My hat's off to my mother
Who always knew I could do it
It wasn't as easy as it looked
There was a lot more to it

Lets not forget my loving wife
Whose steadfast love and care
When she grammar checked my
papers

She left red ink everywhere.

I take a bow at this moment
And pat myself on the back
Tomorrow I move on to new
goals
Lest I be charged with being
slack!

RB^2 The Graduate

Heaven and Earth

What wondrous eyes did I gaze
Into from my crib
The loving hands that changed
And wiped the Gerber from my bib

A reservoir of pure love
That flows so endlessly
That patched the knees and kiss the scrapes
When I fell from that tree

Those loving eyes that watched me grow
To man from the boy you used to know
Those guiding hands that molded me
Into the best man I could be

The heaven and earth's like mother and son
A circle of love united as one
The heaven and earth's like mother and child
Whose joy is found in bright eyed smiles

The lessons taught and happiness brought
Are endless as the days
The love and respect I have you
I'll carry with me always

This love can't be metered
or measured or weighed
If anyone would try it
I'm sure it would break the scales

A mother's love like gravity
That holds us on the ground
Your love's a special love
That makes the world go around

I have often tried to capture
And express this point of view
But in my quest I have found
That words just will not do!

The heaven and earth's like mother and child
Whose joy is found in bright eyed smiles
Heaven and earth's like mother and me
The branches of life on our family tree.
RB[2]

Bridges

We burned those
    bridges,
      that led to   places in the heart,
where thoughtless   comments
cut like   straight razors
    through   sensuous flesh.

B*tch,
    Wh*re,
    invitations to as*es kiss! Motha's-fu*ked!
Me, you,   Who?
    Rivers reflected   the pain.
    Pain I never   wanted you to feel.

We tear down   pillars
    that   held up bridges
while we   cross the rivers
of life, once together,   now separate.
    Wet,
    we drown,
waded   too deep,
    in streams   where bridges
    once were,
east shore,   west bank.

Cold,   we shiver,
    our teeth   chatter with
    the
damp hatred that seeps   through our bones.

$$RB^2$$

Finding Frank L.

Where did you go? Juanita's baby boy.
Somewhere along the way
You slipped and fell, wandered off the path, to a place where
angels and demons devoured you feet first.
Giving you an insatiable thirst for spiritual liquidation
You used to be sooo fine, sooo fly, the bomb
six feet one, size 10 triple A's
Gangsta ride, accompanied, not by flash or bling,
but the real thing
The girls whistle at you through perfect teeth
And you… flashed them your golden smile
That spun into magical laughter
The razor sharp wit that remains intact today
An answer for every problem or dream or desire
My hero, all the things I was not in 1964, or 74
I can't remember which
Only that I wanted to be just like you
when I grew up.
Fast forward to the turn of the century.
After years in government bondage
That I put you in and never knew it
You arrived with your baggage,
the pine box you slept in, draped
in stars and bars.
I still cannot find you
The spirit that made us
All feel like we could swim
The width of the pool at the deep end
With your encouragement
Even though, you could not swim.
Did losing your friend cause you to lose yourself?
Is that what started it all?
Fear of dying or the emptiness of loss?
And all the while you ignored our pleas
To come in out of the rain
Before you catch your death of cold
And even though we fear owning you
And the problem you have become.
We still say, come, sit, eat,
stay awhile, relax,
make yourself at home.
RB^2

50

Tick... Tick...

In the land of milk and honey
forsaken by hope
you, the dead, walk among the living
oblivious to your ulterior motive (tick... tick...)
to take their breath away
for your mythological salvation
(tick... tick...)

You, the have knots... who think you
have more means... motive...
opportunity... reason enough to
self-destruct in the name
of your God (tick... tick...)

Journey through killing fields of fire
laced with laughter, and love and tears
without regard for the pulse of life...(tick... tick...)
radiant light, lit by innocence and warm smiles
observed through eyes of cold copper and steel
searching for a place, warm and fuzzy **(tick... tick...)**
to kiss yourself good night.

Your heart beats louder than the voices
inside your head, mind numbnessly racing,
muscles torqued with anticipation
(tick... tick!!!!)
as you obliterate the dreams of children
change the course of lives in unspeakable ways.
Humanity screams in pain
regarding your selfless act of unkindness.

And through the smoky darkness, agony and pain,
(Your last creation), the sun still rises,
the earth still rotates on its axis at 23 and a half degrees...
never understanding what drove you
to this madness...

RB^2

Younger Daze

We… were eager young lovers she and I,
made radiant love under crystal clear blue sky.
Dancing, finger popping in early morning light,
barefoot in the sand, with fanfare and delight.

Started life together in that city by the sea,
explored the Spanish ruins, saw all there was to see.
Young loving conquers all, so optimistic and fresh,
sparkling, like beach sand in the sun, such memories to
relish!

Dark clouds and rainy days, were few and far between,
and when they came along, still, no season to be mean.
We added up the pain and it divided by two,
dawned our sunglasses, somehow the rays came through.

Time, has handed us
some of life's bitter pills,
two hearts that were as warm as fire,
has taken on an Arctic chill.

We had it made, in that city with the shade,
invincible, inseparable she and I.
The tides of youth have ebbed.
How bleak the sky…

RB^2

Revolution

We need a revolution,
a revolution of the mind.
To save us from ourselves
cause we are running out of time.
Re-think the way we're living
turn this mean old world upside down,
and in it's place on every face,
put a smile instead of a frown.

We need to put a stop to
babies makin babies, and killing.
The only way we're gonna do it,
is if everybody's willing.
To take a giant step towards mankind,
be kind to one another, treat the sisters
like our sisters and our mothers & brothers
like we want to be,
there can be no substitute to this recipe.

We gotta re-think this thing,
in ways that are not so new,
just get back to the basics and
do'em the way we used to do.
The revolution has got to come
before the end of the century,
or the only place we find piece
or pleasure, will be on TV.

We gotta get rid of the blues
on the 7,6,5 O'clock news,
stop letting the media jerk us
around, like we're in the circus.
Change must come from within,
it must come from without,
our focus must be on we'ism
instead so much on me'ism

We need to educate and cohabitate,
eliminate these superficial walls,
learn to share, and love and care
for this world that belongs to us all,
RB^2

REQUIEM

Sweet Sorrow in the Morning

Losing Mom

Losing mom, I feel like I just don't belong
To anyone, to anywhere, everything seems wrong
Like being lost in the woods or moving far away from
home
No matter where I am I feel alone.

Losing mom, makes my heart ache like I never knew it
could
A deep enduring pain that seems never to subside
A pain that comes and goes like the changing of the tide
And tears still flow from my saddened, weary eyes.

As I travel alone through the five stages of grief
I find no peace nor do I find any relief
All my hope is gone, there's no sunny daze
What a terrible price to pay but we all got to pay.

Mom, was my one true treasure
The metric by which all others I measured
Though her stature was small she stood 10ft tall
With a heart big enough to love us ALL

Where will I ever find her love again?
Only in heaven if I stay away from sin
Is that God's promise to us?
Or did we just make this all up?

Death came like a thief in the night
And in the latest hour she went without a fight
Was she saying goodbye all the time and we just didn't
know?
Why did she have to go?

RB[2]

Remembering Frank

I'll remember Frank…
The warm baritone voice
thick with magnolias and palms
that said just what he thought.

The man's man…
Who spoke of love in tough terms
Yet, so protective of the young, the tender.
The way he carried the long fat cigar
Its aroma, only his nose could love.

I'll remember, the master craftsman
Who kept the walls from falling down
On many lives.
Brick, mortar, trowel, level, scaffolding to
heights of self awareness and sacrifice that led
me to… enlightened thoughts as well.
Lone spirit, forged in steel
unshakable character.

Though spring had sprung
the winter of his years blazed into a
quiet fire, a private war inside.
His sun sets on
A life filled with… simple accomplishments
Things built – people, walls, foundations, structures.

And at day's end
The working hands with fat fingers folded behind his head
And in the comfort of familiar surroundings
He went to sleep.
Leaving us to ponder images of his strength and the frailty of his
wisdom.

It's not hard to imagine him smiling now
Maybe with his newly acquired halo and flowing white robe
building some structure of gold and
voicing his… unsolicited opinion.

RB^2

To Ernest and Debbie on the loss of their son Bryan

I don't know what it is like to lose a child
But I feel your pain just the same
Especially one you have nurtured and nourished
For 14 years and without reasonable explanation or expectation they are gone.

I can imagine that he was warm and happy and bright
One of the lights of your life, As all children are
Naive to the ways of the world
With so much promise and hope.

I trust that, in time your pain will subside
and the void that once was will be replaced
with fond memories of his existence.

They say, the best way to remember someone
is to emulate them, some word they used to say or thing they loved to do.
Recalling adventures, situations and circumstances that you were involved in.
You do it. And they will live forever in you.
RB[2]

For Darius Turhan Batie

The pitter patter of your little feet were never heard
and you have never spoken a single word
yet, you left your footprints on all our hearts
we are so sorry that you departed

The little boy we never really got the chance to love
for reasons known only to God above.
Who would you look like?
What would you turn out to be?

An infinite number of possibilities
A separate branch on our family tree.
Though your swift existence has caused great pain
your struggle to survive will not be in vain.

We can and will be better because you were here
We will strive for perfection and hold your memory dear
Your mother knew you better but God knows you best
On this day, April 30, 1996 we lay your little body to rest.
We had so many plans for you!
RB[2]

16 April 16

That night you came and went so quickly
So tiny and helpless
I remember it so clearly
Alone in our room
Just you and I
I held you so close
And I prayed to the sky
Tear filled eyes
And a broken soul
As you passed from this life
Only a few hours old
There's not a day in my life
Where I don't think of you
And how life would have been
If you had pulled through
Your sister talks about you
Almost every day
She understands you're in heaven
Looking down on her play
She asks me what happened
Wants to know what went wrong
To ease her heart and mine
I tell her God wanted you home
April 16th
Approaching so fast
Who knew the pain of that day
Could this long last
I send a kiss and a prayer
To the sky up above
My thoughts are still with you
And so is my love.

Happy eighth Birthday!
Darius
I miss you
Love, Mommy

JDB

Another Summer without You

It happened in the month of June
And here is where our sadness looms
The constant heat, the sporadic rains
the measure of our joy and pain.

As June arrives for the third year
To warm the heart we hold so dear
Who would have thought the time would pass
We never thought the pain would last.

June our nemesis, June our friend
The beginning of your life and ultimately its end
That summer day is crystal clear
The day we faced our greatest fear.

It was the day the music died
We all came home and cried and cried
It was the day the hurt began
A hurt we could not comprehend.

We gather at your resting place
To wipe our tears and reminisce
On how you loved us one by one
And how your touch is truly missed.

Remember how we used to dance?
Remember how we laughed and sang?
Remember how the time would pass
from summer, to fall, to winter, then spring?

And here we stand in summer's daze
to celebrate with family and friends
The life you lived was not in vain
the joy you gave outweighs the pain.

RB[2]

For Elise

Sister, sister, how could I have known,
Today you'd be here with me, and tomorrow you'd be gone.
Sister, if you're listening here is what I want to say,
I'll miss your laughter and your touch and the inspiring things
you'd say.

It never crossed my mind that your time would be so near,
you leave me with only memories and I will always hold them
dear.
You have moved on to that most sacred place
Where dreams are as real as God's loving grace.

I can be better because it was my life you touched
Much deeper than the skin but still not nearly enough.
We had such great plans of visits and girl talk,
Of shopping expeditions and gentle evening walks.

The pain I feel right now, this pain is so intense
I'll be missing my best buddy and it doesn't make much sense.
I know God's plan is the master plan, and your time is your own,
Life's no good without you, I feel so all alone.

RB^2

Our Heart and Soul

We've lost our dear sweet Helen
She was our heart and soul
Yet we were the joy for her heart to behold.

Ironic as it may seem
Never in our wildest dreams
Did we fathom losing our queen of queens.

'Cause day in and day out
She was always there for us without a doubt
Flowing simple love and pearls of wisdom
From her small, yet enormous spout.

Gentle hands that rocked the cradles and our worlds
Musical laughter that enchanted 4 boys and 2 girls
Sweet music that still lingers in our hearts and minds
We never tire of its sound though we've heard it a million
times.

She was our champion, our mother and our friend
She touched the lives of those she loved much deeper than
the skin
In ways we were familiar with yet fail to comprehend.

Sleep on sweet mother, we'll find you in the morning sun
With comforting thought of knowing your journey's just
begun
When dark and cloudy days appear you are the gentle rain
Our hearts find peace in knowing that you're with the king
of kings.

RB[2]

Brown Shoes

Before my Daddy died he gave me these shoes
I put them on when I get the blues
It was the last thing he gave me
Sometimes, they are the only thing to save me.

I put them on and its like Christmas day
I lace them so tight the tongues hide away
These old shoes are size thirteen
I spit shine them until they sparkle and sheen.

They are large and comfortable like my Daddy's love
So they don't fit as snug as a hand in a glove
They flip and flap and flop around
And make my feet look as big as clown's.

I'm growing into them inch by inch
I like the size cause my toes don't pinch
I wouldn't trade these old shoes for nothing I know
Except for a chance to see my Daddy once more.

RB^2

In Lovin' memory of Liz Calhoun

The hands that did the work of god,
A heart that loved us big and small,
No task too great nor distance far
To guide the young toward heaven's star

Your gentle smile embraced us all,
Your sincere passion tore down the walls
To bridge the gap of faith and doubt,
Is what your life was all about

You changed the lives of those you touched,
In ways we did not comprehend.
Saint Cyprian's children miss you much
Our faithful and most gracious friend.

RB^2

Our Grief in Five Stages

The night we lost you
    someone pointed us towards
        the Five Stages of Grief
            it's easy, like learning to climb
                stairs after an amputation.
                    Go that way, they said
                    And so, we
                        climbed.
                          Denial
                    was first.
        We worked all week preparing for our final visit
Going through your papers and things, receiving guests
      making decisions as if you were just
        out of town on business or vacation.
                Anger seemed so familiar but not at you
                    it was him I was mad with
                      Then when I saw how pretty you
          looked
            I wasn't mad any more, just helplessly
        lost at the realization of your departure
and so, I moved on to
Bargaining. What could I exchange
      for you? The silence after storms? My typing fingers?
          The yo-yo you bought me for absolutely no reason
              except that I liked the way it lit up as it
                traveled up and down its solitary
                string?
        Before I could decide, **Depression**
    came knocking like a broke cousin
you have to put up for a while,
      while they try to get themselves together
        suitcase tied together with string
          Bringing only bandages for the eyes
            and bottles of sleep.
             I slid all the way down the
          stairs then, feeling nothing.
      And all the time **Hope**
    flashed on and off
    in Japanese neon.
Hope was a signpost pointing
    straight in the air,
      Hope was what grandma always had…
      she died with it.

After 5 years we are (I am) still climbing,
though our feet slip
on gentle rocks etched
with the impression
of your face.
The forest is still there but
green is a color I have forgotten.
And, now I see what I am climbing
towards: **Acceptance**
written in capital letters,
like the
Woolworth sign
on King Street.
Acceptance
its name in lights.
We struggle on,
waving and shouting and soaring.
Below, my whole life spreads its surf...
all the landscapes we've ever known
or dreamed of, below,
acceptance. We finally reached it.
a fish jumps... it's a dolphin, your favorite.
But something is wrong.
Grief, is a circular staircase.
We have lost you but... we still
love you...
And always will, no matter how many
times we travel up and down these stairs.

RB^2

New Again, Blue Again

New again, blue again
Flowers kiss the dew again
Rain that falls, the voice that calls
It's music heard by one and all
Nourishing, flourishing
Juneteenth has new meaning.

Sunshine pours out on the earth
Completes the cycle of rebirth
Hands that made the plant life thrive
Taught the CRAITS how to survive

Words that forged a beam of light
Moonglow guides us through the night
Constellations etched so clear
The heart we hold so dear

Butterflies fluttering
Quiet times draw us near
Synchronizes all our tears
Squelched the thirst that fed our fears

The spiral staircase seems complete
We forge ahead and not retreat
Our memories' space will not delete
The stories of our past.
RB[2]

Four-Get-U-Not

The morning breeze and warm sunshine
Made for the perfect day
And afternoon a thunderstorm
Struts in and strolls away

And here we stand beneath the sun
Another year had come to pass
We pause once more for Helen G
To emphasize our love, steadfast

Our thoughts will never flicker like
A dying candle's flame
We proudly want the world to know
Our love remains the same

We think of you in all we do
You are in our prayers and dreams
Our feelings range from joy to pain
It's been too long it seems

We miss your lovely smile
And your gentle soothing touch
We miss your words of wisdom, Mom
We miss you very much

While some have wandered aimlessly
And others stayed on task
The lessons of love you taught us
Seem to last and last and last

While seasons change quite rapidly
From cool to warm to hot
In our hearts and minds and soul
The CRAITS Four-Get-U-Not

RB[2]

For Security Reasons...

For security reason...
We are shifting our priorities...
Staying the course...
Giving up the right to be
Safe and secure in our own persons
By default or proxy,
Agreeing to be X-rayed, and medal detected.
Our dirty laundry, weary from traveling
plundered, picked through
And picked apart left with a friendly reminder that
TSA was here, protecting and serving you up
For security reason...
We dare not ask why or who?
Or disagree with the authority
For fear of being Abu Ghraib'ed or
Guantanamo Bay'd.
We relish instead for, phone taps,
And data mines
Privacy scattered into bits and bytes
Identity stolen, to the highest bidder
Bold enough to sell us
that which we already own.
We are over-exposed to terror like sunlit film
faint images
Of what remains of our shattered nerves.
Haunted by those whom we should
be protected from for security reasons...
we boast of security measures as effective as
wearing a seatbelt during a plane crash
For security reasons...
There are no legitimate reasons
For this incompetent administration to
Bull shit us with fabrications and lies
Scandalously squander our resources
Fattening their pockets and the pockets
of their corporate friends
With the spoils of a rigged election and concocted wars.
Who's the real target?
Preying on instead of praying for
Those who are desperately in need of
Winter heating oil or loved ones sent into battle
For security reasons...

RB²

67

Gestation of a New Life

Gestation of a New Life

Late summer, early fall...
The first signs were uncertain ones – discomfort, weird, indescribable
Emotions that pushed me into an unknown space
It fluttered and twitched, did not kick...
What is going on with me?

It kept developing, growing, something attached to me
Kept me awake some nights, fighting for my attention
I struggled with its source but was afraid to ask the Doctor

Thanksgiving... I came to grips with it --- I am pregnant
Could it be that I am connecting, willing to show affection and provide
a lifeline for it?
I faced the truth with a little trepidation, but strong realization that life
is going to change for me, will somehow never be the same again

All that is old and heavy, worn and ill-fitting is being exchanged for
New attire, lightweight garment, fresh, crisp linen, smooth silk, soft
cashmere, supple leather
Tailored to fit perfectly – my new shape

It grows and I grow with it
It kicks and tosses and turns, forcing giggles from my throat some days
Backaches, flesh and emotions tender to touch on others
I am happy with my new condition
Yeah, I'm pregnant, pregnant with joy and love for the seed
The seed He planted in me upon conception
Pregnant with more than hope – with realization, understanding,
openness and willingness
Not with a dream but with an unveiling of life... my belly is growing
I'm comfortable most days, still facing a few cautiously, influenced by
The unknown of beautiful things to come

Still pregnant but preparing for a new birth
A new birth of life, passion, joy, awakened spirit
Outstretched arms resting on my protruding belly
It's still growing... I will deliver soon and slowly – one day at a time
With open arms embracing a new birth
The birth of who and what God wants me to be
Free, truly and completely free.
LKB

WRT: Gestation of a new life

The vicarious thrill of your dreams touched me deeply
Much deeper than thoughts, wandering aimlessly through space
In search of reality
Through the fog and the haze of misplaced emotions
Galvanized by their metaphoric lyricisms
That lights the way with the fragrance of moonlight
And the beauty of the shape of things to come
I am your partner in la maze, I will help you stay focused, to
breathe
Short puffs of air while you labor through this generation of life
Place a pillow at your back when the burden of pregnancy
becomes unbearable
Message your bunion-less feet, sore from pacing back and forth
on sleepless nights
Wipe the sweat from your brow, encourage you to push and push
some more
Both physically and mentally
Until this new life escapes it's birth canal and breathes on its
own
Together we will nurture the infant being
Bring it warm bottles milk and something Gerber
Taking hold with baby steps, unsure at first, then steady
And one day standing, walking and running on its own
We will smile at the thing we created from small seeds and eggs
So much like us but more like you in everyway
Smart, determined, impatient yet graceful and full of
understanding
This body of work will not define you but will be defined by you
Forged with the hammer and anvil of your magnificent creativity
Boarded the train, no turning back!

RB^2

A flashy salesman

A flashy salesman
In a cheap suit
And an expensive watch
Come knocking on my heart
Slick talking m*tha f*cka
Had me sold on tales of
Love and romance
Weekend escapes
In exotic places
Getting to know
Every aspect of my being
And loving every part of me
Truth and honesty
Treating my heart like precious jewels
Deep from African earth
The kinda love
Only fairy tales knew
And I spent every red cent I owned
I begged borrowed and stole
So that I would no longer have to
Use my imagination
Dissecting past encounters
With various other cheap suited salesmen
Selling the same ****
Different brochure
Convinced me
What he had to offer
Was like no other
100% satisfaction guaranteed
The Presentation was immaculate
Conversation articulate
And eyes so sincere
So I bought that ****
Like rich men buy land
And the sex addict buys pu**y
Anybody with some common sense

Knows to read between the lines
And the fine print
But it was late
And I was tired of being lonely
Of course he came with a warning label
Encircled in gold
SHYYYYT
I didn't care
There's always a risk
To get to the reward
Had to go through some sh*t
But I didn't want mine in dollars
I wanted my riches in love
I just didn't know how much risk was involved
Though all my problems was solved
I'd bought the pleasures of heaven
And all I got was hell
Now I'm broke
And broken-hearted
Looking jack-ass-ihs
Hind sight is 20/20
Lawd if I have to go through this
One mo Gin Imma lose it
I tell you what the next time
A slick talking salesman comes knocking
"ME NO SPEAKY ENGRESH"!!!

JDB

Waiting for Spring

The fall year of five and one
I became the chosen one
To battle life in the key of C
A new beginning for me to ponder
A landscape so new and unfamiliar
A path so critical I dare not blunder
A journey that began with a single missed-step
Somewhere in oblivion, totally incognizant
It silently crept.

Through the orchards where angels forged life
Scarred the landscape with its plague
Turned this oasis into a barren land
Bewilderment cried out of ignorance and fear
Envy and jealousy stole all that was dear
But hanging on like static cling
Are rays of hope and the promise of spring.

Beaming to spring's no easy thing
The journey's hard, the battle fierce
A fire fight until the end of life, lock and load
hazard's all around, struggles within
my worst enemy, my best friend
what's the difference…
the darkest night, the brightest day
the blinding sun, the wind and tears.

As random as my choosing may have been
Was it based on salvation or sin?
Must slay the beast that feasts on sacred ground
With rays of hope and the flowers of spring
Spring, when life's renewed
Fertile and abundance fills the air
I have become acutely aware.
There's so much more life to appreciate
An awesome adventure of musical measures
The sound of each step's a sacred treasure
out of the woods, out of the night
and back into the light.
My soul is cleansed, my spirit's at peace
Must pick up the pieces of all that is me
And change my modus operandi

RB[2]

The Trouble with This Place

The trouble with this place is
You are no different from those you replaced
You have yet to earn our respect
Too busy shaping your hidden agendas
Picking your nose and scratching your ass
All the while offering us your vile hand to shake
Vampire smile with blood stained fangs.

The trouble with this place is
You provide no real opportunities
Except for your golden child
The ones who bobble heads
Nod in unison with your evil plans
There are no "Ts" as in equality, diversity or unity
No level playing field with justice for anyone.

The trouble with this place is
There is no trust or honesty only deception and anger
No sanctuary to voice our true feelings
Any attempt to reconcile the dreams of the dreamers
Are met with the reality of retribution
You find joy in squelching the light of enthusiasm
Until all that is left is a Zombie's soul.

The trouble with this place is
All the things you do, you do for you
Actions as transparent as the Arizona sky
When you could have set the eagles free
To soar the thermal currents at heights beyond their dreams
You blindfolded and tethered them to your false sense of security
Crushed their talons
Emphasized the cliques and your common denominators
Of you, for you, like you
Preserved your comfort zone at all cost
Still afraid of the dark?

The trouble with this place is
We will not leave to give you the satisfaction of basking
In your only accomplishment, scorched earth, barren terrain
You are destined to fail because you are not genuine
Your paltry attempts to mingle with the masses
Tickles our funny bones, we laugh in pity
All the while, wishing you were not absent-minded but absent.
Undeniably RB^2

74

What happened to my dream

I wanted to be a star
With my name in bright lights
Driving a fancy new car
Cameras flashing
Fans cheering
My parents would be so proud
"That's my baby"
They would say
With sheer joy in their voices
But my dream faded away
From all of my choices

What happen to my dream
A husband and a wife
A house with a picket fence
Any woman's dream life

My 2.3 kids
And a dog I can't stand
A well paying job
And a wonderful man
Dinners in the evening
House meetings
A loving household
Before it got started
It ended in divorce
That was my choice

What happened to my dream
Although single mother I am
Raising a beautiful little girl
The best that I can
Hoping for the best in this world
For her
She has become
What I have dreamed
She will be greater
And Hopefully
She won't be writing the same poem as me

What happened to my dreams
Of better days
I can have the lights and my family
One in the same
To be happy and whole
Live in better days
I'll tell you why my dreams have faded away
It comes from the choices
That I have made

I see it so clear
And my vision is still blurred
What happened to my dream
I've lost it
Dream is now just a word

JDB

Sundays

Sundays are lazy days I keep to myself
And share with the love of my life
Breakfast that nourishes the soul
As well as food for thought
Intimacy and tender touching
Over scrambled eggs and French
toast
Timeless times
squeezed between
The narrowness of twilight
squinting daylight
and lingering sunsets.

RB^2

Tax Time

Daybreaks, got the blues and the shakes
TuR.Bo tax running, downloading the latest updates
Mind numbing body aches
IRS is coming down on my jock
Round the clock, 5 months to get it straight
15 April is the cut off date
Pay a penalty if I'm late
Only thing I know is true
Stay black, pay taxes and be blue
Feel so bad to be getting Government jacked
So I do the best I can
To squeeze another deduction from the man
Earned income credit, child care, schedule A, D, E
Just an illusion, please Mr. CPA lend a hand
Breaking even would suffice
A 4 digit refund would be mighty nice
Just don't let me owe
'Cause I really don't have the dough
In the end I'll keep it legit
'Cause IRS don't play that shit
They were auditing in 1994
For another chunk of your butt they'll
Be back for more!

RB^2

Princess Di

The princess of Wales, the Queen of hearts
who opened our eyes now shatters our hearts
So young and so pretty, why'd she have to die?
Millions of tears will fall before all eyes are dried.

The hands of inconsiderate, money hungry thugs
are covered in the blood of this lady most loved
The Poparazzi should never be saved
but go straight to hell, in unmarked graves.

Her deep concerns for the humanitarian cause
will forever be remembered with praise and applause
She humbled herself to a low self esteem
The mirrored image in mother Theresa's dreams.

William and Harry her most prized possessions
Will be by her side in this final procession
Somehow they'll survive without mother's clutch
My heart hurts for them 'cause they'll miss her touch.

All who have known her or heard of her story,
knows the way she left in heart wrenching gory
And when it's all over and our pain subsides
who will be next in Poparazzi's probing eyes?

RB[2]

DRIFTING

I've sensed you drifting a long time ago
You've tried to conceal it but still I know
I hoped against all hope that close you would stay
But at long last you're drifting away.

I've pondered and plotted on how to help your life be a
success
But you're drifting away and seem to care less
I've tried to provide you with love and all kinds of stuff
But since you're still drifting I guess it just was not enough.

Oh how I've longed to converse and really get to know you
But you've resisted my attempts and wouldn't let me
through
I can't help but wonder if you'll be all right
It's really a heavy load when you are not in sight.

From day one being there for you even if you didn't call
Daily you're drifting away and it counted for nothing at all
As salty juice flows from my red eyes
I pray this drifting will not result in a tragic surprise.

I knew one day you would leave and maybe travel far away
I'm just sad it happened because things didn't go your way
Few words I'll ever say
But in the center of my heart I know you're drifting away.

CJF

St. Cyprian's Children

When I was a St. Cyprian child
my days were filled with wonder and smiles
That singing choir, those acolytes
as Christian soldiers we learned wrong from right.

St. Cyprian's children are proud as peacocks
smart as PhDs, movers and shakers, humble as pie
family women and men, law abiding citizens
with a Christian light inside of them.

But where have all the children gone?
St. Cyprian's children, had simply moved on
I got up and came to church one day
and none of his children came in to pray.

Some had moved to other towns
while some had heard a different sound
others simply hung around
and just a few could not be found.

The children left an enormous space
in this little church of unshakable faith
Rich with heritage, warmed in God's grace
Their synergy could not be replaced.

To all its children both near and far
this house awaits you, come as you are
to share the wonders of His love is never too late
let us break bread and celebrate.

Those early Christian steps we took
were just a chapter in our lifelong book
And though we travel far and wide
St. Cyprian's children we'll always be with pride.
RB[2]

More Than A Simple Kiss

Books can also be purchased online at Rbbatie.net
or

Geneva Publishing Co.

Please send me a copy (or copies) of

**More Than a Simple Kiss (ISBN 978-0-9790482-0-3)
by R.B. Batie**

Quantity _____ @ $15.00 = _____

Shipping and Handling = _____

Subtotal = _____

Sales Tax (where applicable) = _____

Total Enclosed = _____

Please include $5.00 for shipping and handling for the first book and
add $.50 for each additional book

If you wish to pay by check or money order please make the payable to
RB Batie or Geneva Publishing Co.

If you prefer to use a major credit card please fill out the information
below:

Visa   **Master card**

Account No. _____ **Expiration date** _____

Signature _____

Print Name _____

Address _____

City _____ **State** _____ **Zip Code** _____

Send your payment with the order form above to Geneva Publishing
Co.
PO Box 1926, Lutz, FL 33548-1926

Allow 4 weeks for delivery

82